Studying the Shack
By Dan Phillips

This is a reading group study guide for
THE SHACK
By Wm. Paul Young

Note: for page references, this study guide used the paperback version of the book, copyright 2007, printing series 40 39 38 37 36 35 34

Introduction

I'm just a regular guy that attends a weekly men's group in which we talk about God and some books that we have read. Our group decided to read *The Shack* but we didn't know how we might discuss it. I offered to put together some questions for the chapters we would assign each week, and the group took me up on the offer. Well, one thing led to another and I find myself with a study guide for *The Shack*.

In addition to the questions I came up with, my group encouraged me to include some of my own comments. I want to emphasize that I am just a regular guy. I have no religious training. I teach Sunday School at my church and attend this men's group, that's it. So, please accept my comments as those coming from a person just like you, a lay person.

Hopefully these questions will foster discussion in your reading group. I tend to try to ask direct questions and really count on answers in the first person. To make people feel more comfortable with that approach, and answering out loud to others, small groups tend to work best. I hope that this study guide will provide you with a deeper experience to *The Shack*.

Please note that each question is numbered, then provides a section out of the book (page number, beginning quote and ending quote) before the actual question is presented. Please read the section referred to and then go to the question.

Forward

1. Read:

Page 9   Starting with, "In a world of talkers, Mack is a thinker and a doer." Ending with, "Not too endearing."

AND

Page 10   "He can speak intelligently about anything, and even when you sense he has strong convictions, he has a gentle way about him that lets you keep yours."

Question: What do others think of you when you speak? Do your words bring grace to the moment? Look to Ephesians 4:29.

2. Read:

Page 11   Starting with, "In any case, Mack married up." Ending with, "While Mack's relationship with God is wide, Nan's is deep."

Question: What is the difference between wide and deep when it comes to believing in God? What type of relationship do you have?

Comment

I have found myself, at times, not speaking too well of some people. In my business, I have had experiences with people that may not have my best interest in mind in our dealings, and, some of them have caused me professional harm. When discussions come up about them, I have to try hard do let my words bring grace to the moment.

To me, a wide belief in God relates to having a lot of "book knowledge." A person with wide understanding would be able to open the Bible to page and verse on any topic at hand, for example. On the other hand, a deep relationship means a personal relationship. This type of person will tell you how God works in their life on a day to day basis. This does not mean that they are mutual exclusive. One person can have both.

Chapter 1

1. Read:

Page 16   Starting with, "It took almost a minute to knock of the ice that had already sealed shut the door of the mailbox." Ending with, "And to sign it 'Papa' just made it all the more horrifying."

Question: Is it necessary that God bring you though the most painful times of your life? Meaning, if you did not have God in your heart when you faced difficult times in your life, will God bring you back to those, or similar, moments so that you might experience them again, but this time inviting God to be with you?

2. Read:

Page 19   Starting with, "He would have to wait until Nan made it home before he would get any real medical attention;" Ending with, "He swallowed a couple of over-the-counter painkillers to dull the throbbing and limped toward the front entry."

Question: What are some examples of receiving compensation from trials in your life?

3. Read:

Page 19-20   Starting with, "There was a pause at the other end." Ending with, "'It's okay, I'll just catch Tony some other time, no big deal.'"

Question: Annie has made an assumption that being a Christian, and/or sitting through church, is so bad that one must have to get high to endure it. What are some examples of persecution from non-believers in your life? What do you do to either pre-empt the damage from happening or to set the story straight?

4. Read:

Page 20- 21   Starting with, "'Yup.'" Ending with, "'…how is Kate doing over there?'"

AND

Page 24   Starting with, ""When he finally crawled off the sofa…" Ending with, "…he didn't want Nan included if it turned out to be some kind of cruel joke."

Question: Even when Mack begins to think that (Papa) God is speaking to him, he does not disclose this to anyone. Do you hide evidence of God from others?

5. Read:

Page 21-22   Starting with, "There was a pause and then a long sigh…" Ending with, "'I know.' She sighed, 'I just wish he'd hurry up.'"

Question: Even those intimate with God may find impatience in their prayers to God. What are some examples in your life?

Comment

Later in the book, Papa tells Mack that He might have to try to tell us something 47 times before we finally understand His message. This, too, may be the case with tragedies in our lives. The more pain and suffering, the more blinded we are to try to see the whole picture, to begin to understand what God's plan might include. God is with us when we go through trials the first time, and, He is with us as we relive them in our minds. He wants us to see Him there with us.

Have you ever seen a little kid, perhaps playing in the backyard, who happens to find a really interesting bug, like one of those walking-stick bugs? If they are daring enough, they pick it up. But, every kid will run to tell a sibling or a friend, "Come here! Look what I found!" They want to share the joy of finding something wonderful. Why do adults, when they find something wonderful with God, tend to keep it to themselves? Our relationship with God is to be shared.

Be as patient with God as He is with us. When you submit to the belief that He has a plan for you, you will better understand that what you may pray for you might not yet be ready to receive.

Chapter 2

1. Read:

Page 24-25   Starting with, "Little distractions, like the ice storm…" Ending with, "… - trudging daily through the murky despondency that sucked the color out of everything."

Question: Do you have your own "great sadness" that you bear alone? Become aware of your "great sadness" and the effect it has on your living and the example you set for those in your life. What are some examples of how your burden is seen by others through your actions or words?

2. Read:

Page 29   Staring with, "That evening, as he sat between three laughing children watching one of nature's greatest shows…" Ending with, "He was a rich man, he thought to himself, in all the ways that mattered."

Question: Give some examples in the ways that God's gifts have made you rich?

3. Read:

Page 30   Starting with, "Before it got too late…" Ending with, "…and in his reluctant heart he joined in as best he could."

Question: Do you allow yourself to be drawn to the place where you are closer to God? Or, do you avoid them? Provide some examples. When you do go to that place, so you bring others there as well?

4. Read:

Page 30-31   Starting with, "'Did it really happen?'" Ending with, "…Missy was asking questions that wise people had wrestled with for centuries."

Question: Is God mean?

5. Read:

Page 31-32   Starting with, "'Sweetheart, Jesus didn't think his daddy was mean.'" Ending with, "'No, Missy. He would never ask you to do anything like that.'"

Question: To act as a true believer, a true Christian, are sacrifice and service required? Why?

Comment

If you were to pass away suddenly, right now, have you left things with your loved ones the way you would want them to be? Life is precious, and many times, death is sudden. Ensure that every day, and in every way, you are at a point in all of your relationships that you feel whole. You should not have anybody that you owe an apology to. You should not have anyone waiting for forgiveness. There should be no one doubting that you love them.

You should be so lucky as to have a place that brings you closer to God. It could be a special place, or, it could be a frame of mind during your quiet time. You should be looking forward to meeting God in that place as often as possible. And, you should be happy to share your place with others. This does not mean that other people become a part of your special place. It simply means that you show them that places like this, with God, do exist and help them to secure their own.

Missy died a brutal death. God could have prevented it. By not preventing it, was He mean to Mack? No. God is often easy to blame in circumstances like this. But, I truly believe that He suffers with us, and for us, in times like these. There is evil on this earth. God does not direct evil, but we must learn that it does happen. God endures it with us, and then uses it to better us and our world.

If Jesus lives inside of you, sacrifice and service are not negative words. They are positive actions that bring love to those receiving them and wonderful rewards to those giving them. True sacrifice, giving of yourself to better another; and, true service, doing for others in need, bring such a wonderful feeling that we should be doing these acts all of the time.

Chapter 3

1. Read:

Page 34-35   Starting with, "Sometime during the weekend two other families seemed to magically weave themselves into the Phillips' world." Ending with, "...and both were often together down at the Ducette campsite helping Vicki with J.J."

Question: Have you experienced times, when all is happy, when you are sharing God's creations with no cares, that more people are drawn to you? That you allow more people into your experience? How can you recreate those situations?

2. Read:

Page 36   Starting with, "'This is one of those rare and precious moments...'" Ending with, "...and kissed her on her forehead."

AND

Page 39   Starting with, "As he sat mesmerized by the fire and wrapped in its warmth, he prayed..." Ending with, "...but within twenty-four hours his prayers would change, drastically."

Question: Do you take the time, during the busy day, to cherish those you love? To thank God for your riches? Is the last of your prayers at night a thank you to God for all you have?

3. Read:

Page 37   Starting with, "'She helps people think through their relationship with God...'" Ending with, "He searched quickly for a short answer to Jesse's interest"

Question: When people see that you have a relationship with God, that you are a Christian, they will ask you about your faith. Do you have an answer ready for them?

4. Read:

Page 41   Starting with, "Mack surfaced, yelled at Kate to swim to shore…" Ending with, "…freeing Josh from his tether."

Question: What role, if any, did God play in this instance?

5. Read:

Page 42   Starting with, "Somehow they all made it to shore." Ending with, "…emotions suddenly freed from behind a dam of pent-up guilt and fear."

Question: How would you have reacted to Emil in this situation? Describe what it takes to react the way Mack did?

Comment

What's the old saying? "You can attract more flies with honey than vinegar!" People will be more attracted to you, more interested in you, when you are happy, chin up, smile on your face, and light in your eyes. Being with God makes you that way.

When people see you have Christ in your life, they will both be drawn to you and ask you about it, in some way or another. It's best if you are prepared to answer their questions. Having some answers prepared is great. But, you will also need to be sensitive to the question. Be prepared to listen carefully. God is presenting you with an opportunity to introduce Him to this other person, you have to be empathetic enough to respond in the language that they are both comfortable with and will understand, while not being threatened.

Empathy is a big part of life with Jesus. In order to sacrifice or to serve, you must know what the other person is in need of. Your gift to them can't be from your own desires or thoughts or wants. Your gifts need to be tailored made to each individual in the place and time of the moment. The gift from you is all about the other person.

Chapter 4

1. Read:

Page 44	Starting with, "Six shower stalls and no Missy." Ending with, "'…Oh God, please help me find her?'"
Question:	What would your prayer be at this time? Would it be different? What would be the tone of your voice?

2. Read:

Page 46	Starting with, "It was slow, methodical work, much too slow for Mack…" Ending with, "He was desperate to get Missy back, and surely God knew where she was."
Question:	Is promising things to God dumb and irrational? Do you find yourself making deals with God?

3. Read:

Page 48	Starting with, "As he finished speaking, as if on cue, two patrol cars pulled into the campgrounds." Ending with, "A young man who looked to be in his late twenties introduced himself as Office Dalton, and began taking their statements."
Question:	Why is it important to Mack to note that Office Dalton appeared so young? Many times we judge someone, and their capabilities, on initial impressions. Due to his duress, has Mack already doubted Dalton's abilities? Do you judge people (too soon)?

4. Read:

Page 49   Starting with, "Again he turned back to his assigned task, but nothing seemed to be different than what he remembered." Ending with, "He snapped to awareness as if someone had opened smelling salts under his nose."

Question: Mack knew his daughter, and of her interests and activities, well enough to determine that a red crayon was missing and a ladybug pin was added. How well do you know significant others in your life? How much detail of the life of a loved one do you know? How much does God know about yours?

5. Read:

Page 53   Starting with, "As he listened to Dalton's conversation with Special Agent Wikowsky…" Ending with, "God, how could this happen?"

Question: Find the line, "…of good and evil all mixed up together…" Describe what this means to you. Is there good and evil in this life here on earth? Why is there evil and who controls it? Why do bad things happen to good people?

6. Read:

Page 54   Starting with, "Reporters, with their photographers in tow, began showing up during the morning." Ending with, "…knowing the exposure could go a long way to help in the search for Missy."

Question: Often in times of trouble, grief and despair, you will need to face other people, some friends, some you may never know. How should you present yourself? As a Christian, how should you appear to others? What would non-Christians say about you and your faith in difficult times?

7. Read:

Page 55   Starting with, "When it became clear that the need for their assistance was winding down, the Madisons packed up their own site…" Ending with, "…until she was settled enough to walk to the waiting car."

Question: As the Madisons leave, it is Sarah that calms Nan. As the Ducettes leave, it is Nan that settles Vicki. Where does that calmness, that strength, come from? How is it so easily transported from one being to another?

8. Read:

Page 56   Starting with, "The FBI entourage arrived mid-afternoon from field offices in three cities." Ending with, "…no one questioned his presence at even the most intimate of conversations or debriefings."

Question: Mack was able to be included in typically "police only matters" with Officer Dalton, and now, he is included in FBI debriefings as well. What is it about his personality, or demeanor, that has these officials ignoring protocols?

9. Read:

Page 56   Starting with, "After setting up their command center at the hotel…" Ending with, "Mack believed her."

Question: Would you agree that the act of touch, the act of Wikowsky grabbing Mack's hand in hers and looking him in the eye, was an act of empathy? How did this make Mack feel? Is empathy a form of love? Is empathy a conveyance of God's love through us?

10. Read:

Page 60   Starting with, "By now he had only one prayer left..." Ending with, "Tears traced their way down his cheeks and then spilled off onto his shirt."

Question: What is Mack really asking God? Would your prayer be any different? At this point, are you still with God, or against Him?

11. Read:

Page 63   Starting with, "Wikowsky must have signaled the others because..." Ending with, "On the floor by the fireplace lay Missy's torn and blood-soaked red dress."

Question: Where is God in this part of the story? Has Mack asked God to be a part of his suffering? In your times of despair, do you invite God to be there with you?

12. Read:

Page 65   Staring with, "The tragedy had also increased the rift in Mack's own relationship with God..." Ending with, "...but he felt guilty about these/"

Question: In this passage it states that Mack "tried to embrace a stoic, unfeeling faith." Why? What did he get from this pretense?

13. Read:

Page 65   Starting with, "So when Mack received the note from Papa telling him to meet him back at the shack..." Ending with, "But then why was it signed Papa?

Question   Why the shack?

14. Read:

Page 65-66   Starting with, "Try as he might..." Ending with, "Especially an expensive one bound in leather with gilt edges, or was that guilt edges?"

Question: Do others influence your relationship with God? Is there doctrine that prevents you from direct communication with God? Need there be any difference in the ways in which God communicates with us based on time?

15. Read:

Page 66   Starting with, "But in spite of his anger and depression..." Ending with, "Yes, Mack wanted more, and he was about to get much more than he bargained for."

Question: Does God love screw-ups like Mack? Mack wanted more; what does he really want? What do you want with God?

16. Read:

Page 43   "Sadness is a wall between two gardens – Kahlil Gibran"

Question: Where is the first garden? Where is the second garden?

Comment

I have had people try to explain how one should talk with God, or pray. To me, that seems more like a wide relationship. I find myself talking with God, with a high degree of reverence most of the time, as I would with anyone else. I cry, I laugh, I emote. I figure that God sees through my words to what I really feel anyway. I don't think that it is bad to express anger at God, I think He understands. I do think that He is one of our relationships that we need to make sure that we are up to date on, that there is nothing lacking or wanting, that we have kept our relationship current.

Is it just the human condition to always be judging? We are all guilty of it. Judging other people's clothes, that then leads us to predetermined judgments of personality. Judging might be a derivative of expectations. We form expectations of how each of us should act or perform under circumstances (seen through our eyes) and then judge people according to those expectations. Love should have no expectations, nor judgment. Love should be a continuous activity, not a stop and think moment that then sets the course of our actions.

How well do you know your loved ones? If your love is truly action then you participate in the lives of those you love. In so doing, you are more cognizant of who they are and what takes their interests. If your love is simply a statement you might find that you really don't know that person; that you love only an impression of who you think they might be. You should be able to tell if a loved one was missing a red crayon.

If Jesus lives in you, then you can pass Jesus on to other people. The methods of communication are many. One of those methods is simply touch. You can impart the strength of God through your touch. And, what is really neat, that strength can then be passed from one person to the next, many times made stronger simply by the sharing.

Many people will tell you that they pray to God more often in bad times then in good times. However, I wonder how many people are with God in the midst of anguish? How do you relate with God in the throes of despair? Sometimes you will find a story in which a person has remained strong, both in their outward appearance and demonstratively in the relationship with God during their worst moments. I only hope, if ever faced with such a situation, that I can hold strong with Jesus in me. I don't want to establish a false front to those around me, nor with Jesus in me. Perhaps easier said than done, but if faced with a time as this, I hope that I can find the people in that story that need to see God through me, as I see Him then, a God of love.

I grew up in a church where my perception was that in order to speak with God, I had to go through a priest. And, in order to hear from God, His word would be passed down to me through a priest. This resulted in my reality of leaving that church, and a relationship with God, for many years. I urge everyone to establish a direct communication with God, with Jesus, with the Holy Spirit. You must communicate often. You must understand that God loves you no matter what you've done, no matter where you are on the path of your life. As a friend once said to me, "I speak with God often so that when He calls me, I recognize His voice."

Chapter 5

1. Read:

Page 67-68   Starting with, "Secretly, he began to make plans to travel to the shack the following weekend." Ending with, "…and so doing would just lead to questions that he was not ready to answer."

AND

Page 72   Starting with, "'So,' Willie broke the silence…" Ending with, "He rolled his eyes."

Question: What is a lie? Is withholding the truth, or even the whole truth, still a lie? Is it alright to "protect" those that you love by withholding the truth? Is Mack lying to Nan? To himself? To God? What would happen if Mack were to reveal everything to Nan?

2. Read:

Page 69   Starting with, "Late Thursday afternoon…" Ending with, "Mack was just relieved that Nan had already left."

AND

Page 82   Starting with, "He now faced another dilemma." Ending with, "…and he was looking directly into the face of a large beaming African-American woman."

Question: How would you prepare to meet God in this situation? How will you prepare to meet God with the baggage and experiences you will live through here on earth?

3. Read:

Page 70-71	Starting with, "Without looking at him, Mack walked to the office…" Ending with, "'All I know is that I need to go back.'"
Question:	How have you presented your personal evidence of God to other people? What conviction of faith, or belief, did you convey?

4. Read:

Page 71-72	Starting with, "'I thought you'd say that…'" Ending with, "…finding it heavier than he had anticipated, and grunted as he hoisted it."
Question:	Mack started this effort with lies. Now, he is going back on personal decisions he made long ago, and is taking a gun with him after much rationalization. When have you begun a period in your life separating yourself from God only to find yourself slipping further and further away from Him, and, the person He wants you to be?

5. Read:

Page 73	Starting with, "'So, what do you think he looks like?'" Ending with, "sort of like Gandalf in Tolkien's *Lord of the Rings*.'"

AND

Page 84-85	"The large black woman gathered his coat and he handed her the gun…" Ending with, "But his eyes and smile lit up his face and Mack found it difficult to look away."

Question:	What will God look like? Does it bother you that God is portrayed as the trinity? Does it bother you that God is portrayed as a black woman; as an Asian woman; as a Middle Eastern man? If so, why?

6. Read:

Page 73	Starting with, "'Well, if he does show, say hi for me...'" Ending with, "He probably could use all the prayers he could get."
Question:	Willie says that he will pray for Mack. Mack replies by saying that he loves him too. Why does Mack say, "I love you too?" How does someone else praying for you help you?

7. Read:

Page 74-75	Starting with, "He retraced the same path they had taken three and a half years before..." Ending with, "'Please help me!' he groaned."
Question:	Mack is on a journey back to where his separation from God began. Is this an easy journey? Why must it be done? Mack is furious and confused with God, why then does he ask for help?

8. Read:

Page 77	Starting with, "Taking another deep breath and exhaling slowly, he calmed himself." Ending with, "...he was more than ready to get a few things off his chest, respectfully, of course."
Question:	Mack states that he will be respectful, however, does this truly reflect how he is feeling towards God? Is he putting on a front? Doesn't God already know exactly what is in our hearts? Are we better off simply baring our souls to God without any pretenses?

9. Read:

Page 77   Starting with, "A few turns later he stumbled out of
                 the woods and into a clearing." Ending with,
                 "Feeling bolder, he stepped completely across the
                 threshold and stopped."

Question: Is God with Mack? Is Mack leveraging the power
                 of having God in his life, though he has doubts, to
                 overcome the fear he has in coming to the shack?

10. Read:

Page 78-79   Starting with, "And finally his heart exploded like a
                 flash flood…" Ending with, "He spat out the
                 words."

Question: Is this Mack's confession? Has he come to the
                 place where he can be honest with God? Is it wrong
                 to question God this way, or, is it better to let God
                 share your burden?

11. Read:

Page 79   Starting with, "Mack could feel the gun in the small
                 of his back…" Ending with, "Killing himself
                 would be one way to strike back at God, if God
                 even existed."

Question: Have you ever induced self-loathing or harmed
                 yourself to get back at God? What is the root cause
                 of that separation from Him?

12. Read:

Page 79-80   Starting with, "It was probably only minutes later
                 that Mack woke with a jerk." Ending with, "A
                 weary old man, he stepped off the porch and with

	heavy footsteps and a heavier heart started the hike back to the car."
Question:	What did Mack finally do, what did he finally let happen, that will allow him to let him hear God speak with him again?

13. Read:

Page 83	Starting with, "Suddenly, he was overwhelmed by the scent emanating from her, and it shook him." Ending with, "It was warm, inviting, melting."
Question:	Obviously, God knows Mack. But, is God so much a stranger to Mack? God asks Mack to "go ahead and let it out," but Mack was not ready to let it go, "not with this woman." Has Mack been separated from God for so long that he doesn't know Him when he hears God speak?

14. Read:

Page 85-86	Starting with, "The man then stepped in, touched Mack on the shoulder..." Ending with, "...did he realize that he was still standing on his feet and that his feet were still touching the deck."
Question:	What did the Middle Eastern man do that made Mack instantly like him? What did the Asian lady do that made Mack feel lighter than air? If the love of God, and if the Holy Spirit, both reside in you, what will your touch do to others? Do you touch other people with the love of God?

15. Read:

Page 87	Starting with, "Thoughts tumbled over each other as Mack struggled to figure out what to do." Ending with, "...so he focused on the one question he most wanted answered."

Question: Has any bias you may have prevented you from really seeing God?

Comment

A lie is a sin. A definition of sin could be an act that begins the separation between you and God. A definition of a lie could be a statement that requires another statement sometime in the future to cover up the first statement. Once you begin to lie, you begin to separate yourself from God. That path is perilous and slippery. You need to recognize this path you have chosen quickly and make amends, confess your sins, as soon as you can to have Jesus rest comfortably within you.

God knows your heart, and your mind. He is tending your soul. When it comes time to communicate, it is our own feelings that prevent us from fully opening up to Him. Oh, to have a relationship of such love and trust that anger and warmth, ego and humility, and, selfishness and respect, are all spoken and shared as they are felt. That is what God wants. That is what our loved ones deserve. That is how we should treat each other.

There are three thoughts focused on in this chapter. Are you prepared to see God? Are you prepared to share God? And, are you prepared to be with God? Don't let your bias prevent you from seeing God. When you find God, or evidence of Him or His work, share it openly with other people. When you talk with God, be open, be respectful, be comfortable, be yourself.

Chapter 6

1. Read:

Page 88   *"No matter what God's power may be, the first aspect of God is never that of the absolute Master, the Almighty. It is that of the God who puts himself on our human level and limits himself."*

AND

Page 96   "Papa reached for the kitchen timer, gave it a little twist and placed it on the table in front of them."

Question: Did Papa really need a timer to remind Him when the pie would be ready to take out of the oven? In what ways do you put limits on God to better understand Him? Are you aware that you do put limits on God?

2. Read:

Page 88   Starting with, "'Well, Mackenzie, don't just stand there gawkin' with your mouth open like your pants are full...'" Ending with, "...a full arm's length away from her."

Question: In this passage, Papa tells Mack that if he goes fishing, and brings back fish, "you gotta clean what you catch." In Luke 5, there is the story of where Jesus will make His disciples "catchers of men." As a Christian, it is our job to bring more people to God. Is this telling us that not only do we bring people to God, but we also need to clean them? How so?

3. Read:

Page 89   Starting with, "'Really?' said Mack, still shaking his head…" Ending with, "'Go because it's what you *want* to do.'"

Question: What type of relationship do you have with God? Why do you pray? Why do you go to church? Are you obligated, or, do you really enjoy those moments to be closer to God? Do you recognize closeness to God when you have it?

4. Read:

Page 91-92   Starting with, "'You must know,' he offered, 'calling you Papa is a bit of a stretch for me.'" Ending with, "'If you let me, Mack, I'll be the Papa you never had."

Question: Are you able to let God into your heart where the wounds run deepest? Is God waiting for you to ask Him into your life, or to help with one difficult part of your life?

5. Read:

Page 92   Starting with, "'If you couldn't take care of Missy…'" Ending with, "'I want to heal the wound that has grown inside of you, and between us.'"

Question: Is it alright to question God? To be angry with Him? Has God brought Mack back to the worst place in his life to make him relive his loss for a purpose? Do we need to relive our worst moments, with God in our hearts, to mend the wounds between He and us?

6. Read:

Page 93	Starting with, "Mack almost laughed out loud and want to say…" Ending with, "…that all his visuals for God were very white and very male."
Question:	How do you see God? By defining a visual, are we putting limits on God? Does our visual of God show more of our own prejudices than we might want to admit?

7. Read:

Page 94-95	Starting with, "'Then, was I free *not* to come?" Ending with, "'Only I can set you free, Mackenzie, but freedom can never be forced.'"
Question:	What are some of the limited influences in your life that actively work against your freedom? Are you aware of how your decisions are influenced by exterior forces? Is it possible to reduce, or remove, these forces to make your own, free will decisions? What is freedom really? Papa says, "Only I can set you free…" What does that mean?

8. Read:

Page 95	"She turned back and smiled, 'I know. I didn't tell you so that you would understand right now. I told you for later. At this point, you don't even comprehend that freedom is an incremental process.'"
Question:	What incremental steps do you need to take to be free?

9. Read:

Page 95 …"'Mackenzie, the Truth shall set you free and the Truth has a name, he's over in the woodshop right now covered in sawdust. Everything is about *him*. And freedom is a process that happens inside a relationship with him."

Question: As a child, did you have freedom of choice in the relationship with your parents? As a parent, do you offer freedom of choice to your children? In the relationship with your spouse, do you have, or offer, freedom of choice? What is the process that enables freedom as you develop a closer relationship with Jesus?

10. Read:

Page 95-96 Starting with, "Papa didn't answer, only looked down at their hands." Ending with, "'…When all you can see is your pain, perhaps then, you lose sight of me?'"

Question: When are sometimes in your life that you have lost sight of God? What can you do for others, when they are in pain, to help them see that God is still with them?

11. Read:

Page 96 "'Don't forget, the story didn't end in his sense of foresakenness. He found his way through it to put himself completely into my hands. Oh, what a moment that was!'"

Question: How much of yourself do you allow to rest in God's hands?

12. Read:

Page 97   Starting with, "'Consider our little friend here,' she began." Ending with, "'And if left unresolved for very long, you can almost forget that you were ever created to fly in the first place.'"

Question: What situations in your life have you used to clip your wings, to prevent yourself from accepting the love of God? If it is God's intent to love us all of the time, what prevents us from feeling that love all of the time?

13. Read:

Page 98   Starting with, "'I know, honey. That's why we're here.'" Ending with, "'Even though you can't finally grasp me, guess what? I still want to be known.'"

Question: Is God quantifiable? How do you know God? Can you describe Him to someone else?

14. Read:

Page 99-100   Starting with, "'Although by nature he is fully God, Jesus is fully human and lives as such.'" Ending with, "'...'but by everything it means to be created in my image.'"

Question: Papa describes Jesus as "...the first to believe in my love and my goodness without regard for appearance or consequence." Have you ever limited your relationship with God for fear of appearance or consequence? How would you describe your current state of 'co-union' with God? Do others see you as flying, or grounded? If your touch can ease another's pain, how much more relief could you provide if you allowed God to touch them through you? Have you asked God what His intentions are for you?

15. Read:

Page 102   Starting with, "With that, papa stood up…" Ending with, "'As much as you are able, rest in what trust you have in me, no matter how small, okay?'"

Question: Have you ever been left with just a small amount of faith left? Still, are you able to leverage that small amount to trust in God? If you weren't to trust in God, what would you do? And, what would the outcome be?

Comment

Fortunately, and unfortunately, for us God is omni- everything. It is fortunate that we have such a capable and loving God. It is unfortunate because we are unable to grasp and understand everything that God is. In order to think of Him, to picture Him in our minds, perhaps to even converse with Him, we need to put limits on Him for our own sake. The challenge for us is to develop our faith as much as we can so that our understanding of Him transcends what our experiences and knowledge tell us to the point that we just believe, and then act as such.

As a child, we earn more freedom from our parents the better we handle our responsibilities and show maturity. God gives us unlimited freedom of choice. At first, most likely due to ignorance, we misuse those freedoms. However, as we begin to know God better, we should strive to make better judgments, better decisions. We should take the time to listen to the Holy Spirit, to pray with God, before we make choices. Hopefully we can come to a point whereby our decisions are based more upon the love and service to others than ourselves.

God encourages us to become the best person we can become. A major part of that person should include both a positive work ethic and the maintenance of a strong relationship with God. We are not meant to be idle, to sit in our Living Rooms sequestered from the outside world. I dare say that we are not meant to only dwell within the world of our family. We are tasked with expanding the touch of God through us to as many other people that we can. To do this, we need to continually expand our comfort zone and reach out. To help us, a relationship with God will be both a driving force and a positive re-enforcer.

We are to understand that God is limitless. And, that by co-existing with Him in our soul, we can stretch the bounds of our limits. It is fear and evil that clips our wings. A close relationship dims the fear and provides the courage to confront the evil. Don't fall to self-destruction. Let God work through you and make you more in His image.

Chapter 7

1. Read:

Page 105   Starting with, "As he leaned against the doorway watching…" Ending with, "How different this was from the way he treated the ones he loved!"

Question: Describe the relationship that Papa, Jesus and Sarayu have. How different is this from the way you treat your loved ones? How different is this from the way you treat other people?

2. Read:

Page 105-106   Starting with, "Conversation seemed almost normal." Ending with, "'…and we take great delight in seeing them through your eyes.'"

Question: Have you ever spoken with someone that really knows you well, explaining something to them that they probably already know about you, and find that just in the telling you realize something new? How might the thought on God's limitation in conversation with us change your dialogue with Him?

3. Read:

Page 106-107   Starting with, "Sarayu squeezed his hand and seemed to sit back." Ending with, "'…or even in caring for the other who has assumed a position of power over them.'"

Question: Do you find that some of your relationships are defined by who holds the power? Do you really have any relationships that are void of the power struggle? Can one be humble, serve another, and still retain strong self-esteem or self-confidence?

4. Read:

Page 107-108 Starting with, "Mack had to suppress a snicker..."
Ending with, "'Sarayu,' Jesus began softly and
tenderly, 'you wash, I'll dry.'"

Question: If you were sitting at this table, would the devotion
that Jesus spoke about Papa feel corny? Would you
feel uncomfortable with that level of open emotion?
Why? In this passage holiness is defined as,
"simple, warm, intimate, genuine." How might
employing these traits influence your relationships?

5. Read:

Page 109-110 Starting with, "'It certainly is.'" Ending with,
"...'Did you see that? Awesome!'"

Question: Here, something created by God, the stars in the
night sky, is referred to as holy. Does this conform
to simple, warm, intimate, and genuine? Is the state
of holiness something that one portrays, or is it
something that we interpret, or, could it be both?
How do you bring more holiness into your life?

6. Read:

Page 111-112 Starting with, "'I guess I expected you to be
more...'" Ending with, "...-and any appearances
that mask that reality will fall away.'"

Question: How do you see Jesus? If we are created in His
image, is it the outside appearance of each other we
should relate to, or their action of *being*? What
relationships have you experienced where you no
longer cared about the appearance of the other
person? Can you take that same level of
understanding, or love, and put it into your other
relationships?

7. Read:

Page 112-113   Starting with, "'You said I don't really know you.'" Ending with, "'It requires that a very real dynamic and active union exists.'"

Question: How adapt are you at ignoring the concerns of the flesh and enabling the Holy Spirit to dwell within you? This passage states that in order to facilitate this, it takes a "very real dynamic and active union." Describe what this means? What actions are required of you to foster this type of union?

8. Read:

Page 114   Starting with, "'Jesus?' he whispered as his voice choked." Ending with, "…his tension lessened by the words of his newfound friend."

Question: Jesus states that He is not lost. Does this mean that He is never lost in the path that your life will take? Does this mean that no matter when you call Him, He will know where you are and where you are going? Is there comfort in knowing that He already knows the *being* that you will become?

Comment

In this chapter, holiness is defined as "simple, warm, intimate, genuine." Together, those words describe more of a relationship than a thing. These qualities should be adopted into our being. We should be able to portray these to those we love, and hopefully, to everyone we encounter. If that is the case, then we should also be able to see these traits in other people. People living these traits should be attractive to us because they would represent true and honest relationships. People, perhaps not as blessed to show these traits, need relationship with us to give of ourselves those traits to them.

The love of others should bring fullness into your life. The acts of loving, and being loved, should continue to charge your batteries, to rev up your life, to make you wanting to seek more love in more relationships. True love in a relationship has nothing to do with the comparison of power between those in the relationship. We should not care about status of any kind instead we should care about the well being of each other. A great relationship would really be a "very real dynamic and active union."

We were made in the image of Jesus Christ. Many times, the first thought is that we were made to look like Jesus. In reality, we were made to "be" like Jesus. We have the capacity, even with freedom of choice, to love one another. It should be our goal to do just that. If you truly love your spouse, or your parent, or your child, the importance of their appearance in relation to how much you love them should not be a consideration at all. We must carry forward that same kind of love, to where the looks of another person do nothing to bias the amount of love we show them.

Jesus was a very self-confident man. Yet, He sacrificed himself. And, He served those around Him. Sacrifice and service do not mean that we need to be meek or consider ourselves lower in power or status than others. Serving others does not mean that you are lesser than those you serve. I like to think that Jesus was very aware of who He was, loved by God, and that He still chose to serve others and eventually offer the greatest sacrifice. In His image, we should also carry ourselves with honor and high esteem, through the love of God, as we sacrifice and serve others in our world.

Chapter 8

1. Read:

Page 117   Read, "He let out a deep, heavy sigh. And if God was really here, why hadn't he taken his nightmares away?'

Question: Why doesn't God take the nightmares away? Or, are they ours to give to Him?

2. Read:

Page 118   Starting with, "'So, honey,' Papa asked, continuing busily with whatever she was doing." Ending with, "'Is he your favorite? Bruce, I mean?'"

Question: What prevents you from inviting God into "that hole" with you?

3. Read:

Page 119   Starting with, "'But you're asking me to believe that you're God...'" Ending with, "'...instead of trying to fit it into your preconceived notions.'"

Question: What preconceived notions do you have that prevent you from accepting God as He is?

4. Read:

Page 120-121   Starting with, "They passed the food to one another and Mack was spellbound..." Ending with, "Each seemed more aware of the others than of themself."

Question: How can you change your family dinner conversations to be more like this one? How can you inject love, humility and service and take out selfishness, power and disrespect in all of your conversations?

5. Read:

Page 121-122   Starting with, "'Well, I know that you are one and all...'" Ending with, "'...it is almost incomprehensible that people could work or live together without someone being in charge.'"

Question: What is the difference between a *circle* of relationship and a chain of command? How would you start a circle of relationship?

6. Read:

Page 122-123   Starting with, "'It's one reason why experiencing true relationship is so difficult for you,' Jesus replied." Ending with, "'...you end up missing the wonder of relationship that we intended for you.'"

Question: Describe a relationship apart from power. Can a small group of people begin a circle relationship, absent of power, that would spread to more and more people?

7. Read:

Page 123-124   Starting with, "Sarayu continued, 'When you chose independence over relationship...'" Ending with, "'We won't use you.'"

Question: Jesus says that there would be no hierarchy if we had truly learned to regard each other's concerns as significant as our own. Are you able to be this way within your own family? Mack is afraid that without power in a relationship, people will just use each other. Is this true? Is there no way around it?

8. Read:

Page 125   Starting with, "'Mackenzie,' papa answered tenderly..." Ending with, "'...I will use every choice you make for the ultimate good and the most loving outcome.'"

Question: What could possibly be the most loving outcome in the death of Missy?

9. Read:

Page 126   Starting with, "Sarayu spoke." Ending with, "'Because you do not know that I love you, you *cannot* trust me.'"

Question: Is it possible to fake trust? Is it possible to fake humility? If you don't know that God truly loves you, how do other people perceive you? What do they see in your appearance other than in your "being?"

10. Read:

Page 127   Starting with, "'One last comment,' he added turning back." Ending with, "'We are redeeming it.'"

Question: Which definition of "redeem" would you prefer for this passage, and why?
         a) deliver, save from sins
         b) restore the honor or worth of
         c) to turn in and receive something in exchange
         d) to recover ownership of by paying a specified sum
         e) to set free
         f) to make up for

Comment

God is always there with us. He knows everything about us, and about what we are thinking or going to do. When it comes time to confess or to open up to Him, it is our own concerns that prevent it. Pride, ego, shame; all have a part in keeping us separated from God in our private relationship. Add to that, any preconceived notions we might have as to what God is, or how He communicates, or how He might manifest Himself, all prevent us from seeing the true God.

There is an interesting experiment we might try that is highlighted in this chapter. That would be to reform the family conversation at dinner time. If we could truly regard each other's concerns to be as significant as our own, imagine what the conversations would be like. Instead of pretending to care what a child did at school, or dominating the conversation just because you are older, think of the dialogue one could foster by seeing other's concerns as important as our own. You can't fake trust or humility. And, you can't fake interest and empathy either. If a circle of relationship instead of a chain of command be incorporated at dinner time, the stories told and the love shared would be quite wonderful.

Chapter 9

<u>1. Read:</u>

Page 128-129   Starting with, "It was a chaos in color." Ending with, "'But,' she looked back at Mack and beamed, 'it's still a fractal, too.'"

AND

Page 138   Starting with, "Sarayu stepped toward him until she had invaded his personal space." Ending with, "'...I see a perfect pattern emerging and growing and alive, a living fractal.'"

Question: Can you see how your life might be viewed as a fractal from above? By Sarayu's definition, a fractal is "composed of repeated patterns no matter how magnified. A fractal is almost infinitely complex." Think of how your life reflects this definition.

<u>2. Read:</u>

Page 131   "'Oh, Mackenzie, if you only knew. It's not the work, but the purpose that makes it special. And,' she smiled at him, 'it's the only kind I do.'"

Question: What tasks, what efforts, have you put forth realizing that they weren't tiring but rewarding in that only the purpose mattered? How can you do that more often? Where do you find opportunities to work like that?

<u>3. Read:</u>

Page 132   Starting with, "They enjoyed a few moments of silence as Mack looked back..." Ending with, "'...is an act of love that is a gift inside the process of life.'"

| Question: | A child is in a perpetual state of curiosity, always seeking. Have you lost the capacity to be curious? When do you go searching for the secrets that God has hid on this earth; in nature, in science, in relationships, in love? |

<u>4. Read:</u>

| Page 132-133 | Starting with, "Mack gingerly reached out and took the poisonous twig." Ending with, "'Humans have a great capacity for declaring something good or evil, without truly knowing." |

| Question: | Sarayu is telling Mack that humans judge plants (and other things) as good or evil based upon our own interpretations; that we are unable to fathom the real properties in all that was created. That we think that something that is bad, or could be bad, serve no purpose towards good. Does this explain why bad things happen to good people? |

<u>5. Read:</u>

| Page 133 | Starting with, "Obviously the short break, which had been for Mack's sake..." Ending with, "'...then they cannot do what comes naturally and harm the seed we will plant.'" |

| Question: | Is this why God takes us back to relive the painful moments in our lives? To uncover all of the attempts we have made to continue on, to remove them, so that God can plant the correct seeds that will grow and not be hindered by our own attempts? |

6. Read:

Page 134-135   Starting with, "'To be honest,' said Mack… Ending with, "'…and arguments ensue and even wars break out.'"

Question: How do you not judge?

7. Read:

Page 135-137   Starting with, ""'I can see now,' confessed Mack…" Ending with, "'…he opened a door that would allow you to live free enough to give up your rights.'"

Question: Where are you on the scale from independent to a "co-union" with God? Sarayu says that the good may actually be the presence of cancer, or loss of income, or loss of life. Does this answer our question as to why we think that bad things happen to good people? Is having rights the opposite of being a servant? How do you give up one for the other? In a world of love, would it be necessary to stand up for yourself?

Comment

One of the exercises I use when I teach Sunday School is to have the class color their soul. If we assume that we are born with a pure white, unblemished soul, and that as we go through life our experiences leave colorful marks on our soul, then, we would all have uniquely colored souls. So, the Sarayu concept of each life as a garden fractal is quite similar. If life is a series of events tailored so that we can learn the aspects of "being" as Papa and Jesus describe, and that most always we need to repeat the same lessons over and over again, then a representative view of our living could be this fractal.

I have found that when I am truly helping another person my endurance is so high that I feel tireless. However, I have not really taken the step forward to search for more opportunities to feel that good as often as I think I should. One of the men in our study group has though. He told us a story of having to travel to a meeting, which would take about 4 hours by car. He wanted to leave early to avoid the local traffic, but in doing so it would put him at his location hours ahead of the meeting. So, before he left, he found a shelter that used volunteers to man the food line. Arriving hours ahead of schedule, he manned the food line, and then with plenty of energy, went on to his business meeting.

Love is the opposite of judging. In fact, love could be the opposite of most every negative word there is. As humans, how do we get past that first act of judging others to get to the act of loving them? I wonder if, instead of looking at the outward appearances or the behavior exhibited, we first look inside of others to find God. When we look for the presence of God in others, and then find it, that should be the entity that we pursue and foster our relationship with. We must be curious to find both how God is in tune with that other person and to see evidences of the fractal of their life.

Chapter 10

1. Read:

Page 140-141   Starting with, "Mack walked to the edge of the dock and looked down." Ending with, "'I imagine that-'"

Question: What are the fears that prevent you from taking the first step with God? How do you get past them?

2. Read:

Page 141-142   Starting with, "'Exactly,' Jesus interrupted." Ending with, "...God was always absent."

Question: Where do you spend most of your time, living in the present, in the past or in the future? If you are not living in the present, are choosing then not to live with Jesus? When you imagine the future, is God with you? Are you doing the work of God? Are you relating to God?

3. Read:

Page 142   Starting with, "'It is you desperate attempt to get some control over something you can't.'" Ending with, "'You sing about it; you talk about it, but you don't know it.'"

Question: How do we go beyond talking about God's love for us and knowing that God loves us? What has to change inside of us? How would that change be visible to others?

4. Read:

Page 144   Starting with, "'Thank you, Mack, and you've seen so little.'" Ending with, "'...they are offended and raise their fist at God.'"

Question: Is the earth an entity that receives love from God? Are we to love the earth like we are supposed to love each other?

5. Read:

Page 145   Starting with, "'Have you noticed that even though you call me Lord and King...'" Ending with, "'In fact, we are submitted to you in the same way.'"

Question: Jesus says in this passage that to force His will on us is exactly what love does not do; that a genuine relationship is marked by submission, even when choices made by the other are not helpful or healthy. Is this how you raise children? Would children need to mature to a point that they would understand submission and respect? If we are children to God, what maturation process do we need to go through to get to the point that we do not feel as if we are submitting to authority by following God, but that we are in a dynamic, two-way, respectful relationship with Him?

6. Read:

Page 146-147 Starting with, "'You're not just dealing with Missy's murder.'" Ending with, "'...their own quests for power and security and significance, and return to me.'"

Question: If you are a woman, do you have human relationships that have priority over your relationship with God? If you are a man, do you have works that have priority over your relationship with God? What would it take to *re-turn* to a relationship with God?

7. Read:

Page 149   Starting with, "'There it is again,' Mack said…"
                     Ending with, "Mack had no idea what he meant."

Question: What did Jesus mean when He said, "Oh, what
                     could have been?"

8. Read:

Page 149   Starting with, "Jesus just ignored his question."
                     Ending with, "'Time is on our side.'"

Question: Many of us aspire to be Christ-like, to act like Jesus
                     did. Is that just a superficial aspiration? How do
                     we let Jesus live His life inside of us? Are you
                     capable of seeing with God's eyes; hearing with
                     God's ears; and, touching with God's hands?

Comment

This chapter is really all about our relationship with God. It is about faith and being versus thinking and acting. What I took from this chapter is a new thought process. I have been thinking that our goal should be to act as Christ-like as possible. This thought also makes up one of my lessons in Sunday School. Not that it is a bad goal, but, after reading this chapter I realize that it is not enough. Though impossible, our goal should be that our relationship with Jesus is so strong that our state of being is in tune with His state of being. This all starts through love, which blinds us to all that is human and opens our eyes to what is the essence of all.

I have often prayed, "Lord, let me be the conduit through which Your light may shine." Without realizing it, this has put me in a passive position. Yes, I still feel that I do good, but only as a conduit, not necessarily as me. I need to change that to, "Lord, let me speak as You would, let me touch as You would, let me love as You do." This would put more into an active role, a state of being that conveys love.

Chapter 11

1. Read:

Page 154	Read, "'Among the mysteries of a broken humanity, that too is rather remarkable; to learn, to allow change.'"
Question:	What are some of God's lessons that you have learned? Are you able to allow change? What, in you, needs to be changed?

2. Read:

Page 155	Starting with, "She sat back beaming." Ending with, "'…with a wonderful and real love.'"
Question:	What more do you need to *know* about those close to you to expand your love for them? What more do you need to *know* about other people to love them? Explain the line, "Love is just the skin of knowing."

3. Read:

Page 158	Starting with, "'Oh, that is not true,' returned the quick reply…" Ending with, "'By all accounts, you are quite well-practiced in the activity.'"
Question:	List the criteria you use to judge other people.

4. Read:

Page 160-161	Starting with, "'Why not? Surely there are many people in your world you think deserve judgment." Ending with, "'Yes, him too!'"
Question:	Do you agree with Mack? Why or why not?

5. Read:

Page 161   Starting with, "'How far do we go back,
                Mackenzie?'" Ending with, "The accusation hung
                in the room as the gavel fell in his heart."

Question: Do you agree with Mack? Why or why not?

6. Read:

Page 163   Starting with, "'I can't. I can't. I won't!'" Ending
                with, "'...who loves all his children perfectly.'"

Question: When has your love of another cost you anything?
                How did that make you feel? Are you prepared to
                love others when it costs you something?
                Anything? Everything?

7. Read:

Page 163-164   Starting with, "Immediately Missy's image flashed
                in his mind and he found himself bristling." Ending
                with, "'She's not punishing you, or Missy, or Nan.
                This was not his doing.'"

Question: Who is your God? If your god is anything but
                Light, Good and Love, who then are you
                worshiping? Who are you blaming? Who are you
                using as a crutch or an excuse for things gone
                wrong?

8. Read:

Page 164   Starting with, "'But he didn't stop it.'" Ending
                with, "'...and horrible things happen to those that
                he is especially fond of.'"

Question: "The world is severely broken." Individually, are
                we faced with fixing the world? Are we supposed
                to return humanity to God?

9. Read:

Page 165	Starting with, "'But I still don't understand why Missy had to die.'" Ending with, "'Papa has crawled inside of your world to be with you, to be with Missy.'"
Question:	Does God make evil happen in our lives? Does being a believer in God make you immune from evil? When evil happens, where is God?

10. Read:

Page 167	Read, "'More than you know. Life is only the anteroom of a greater reality to come. No one reaches their potential in your world. It's only preparation for what Papa had in mind all along."
Question:	What must we do to prepare? What must you do?

11. Read:

Page 167	Read, "Yes, I am sure,' she assured Mack. 'She has been very excited for this day. To play with her brothers and sister, and to be near you. She very much would have liked her mother to be here too, but that will wait for another time.'"
Question:	Why is Nan not here?

12. Read:

Page 168	Starting with, "'If you remember, you were saving your son.'" Ending with, "'…her love is much stronger than your fault could ever be.'"

Question: What lie do you believe of yourself that keeps you separated from God? As you with your own child, can you not see that God forgives any fault that you might have?

Comment

As a child grows, he matures. In so doing, he changes. We must also change. We must change to actively invite, accept and relate to God in ourselves to create a new state of being. This chapter highlights three areas. One is love over judgment. Again, the theme of love is the opposite of judgment. Second is forgiveness over rights. No matter what the action of another person, there is a history that brought that person to that course. We are not to confuse this with legal issues, which are for the sake of society. Instead, we need to keep our individual perspective. Forgive the person and then love them despite their actions. Last, in every situation there are people directly or indirectly involved who are waiting to see God. It is our task to show them God in our souls.

Chapter 12

Page 170   Starting with, "As Mack way down the trail toward
              the lake, he suddenly realized that something was
              missing." Ending with, "...Despair that had sucked
              the colors of life out of every thing."

Question: With the Great Sadness gone, what will fill the void
              of Mack's identity?

2. Read:

Page 173   Starting with, "'Did she know you were there?'"
              Ending with, "'She was so brave."

Question: How is it that Missy, a six year old, could speak
              with Jesus in time of trouble? How is it that she
              "knew His peace?" How are you different than a
              six year old?

3. Read:

Page 173   Starting with, "The tears flowed freely now..."
              Ending with, "...and blew it out as he lifted his
              head."

Question: Have you ever handed over something terrible to
              God? Do you still have something to hand Him?

4. Read:

Page 174-175 Starting with, "'Thank you for being with me, for
              talking to me about Missy." Ending with, "'...you
              start to see them for what they are.'"

Question: What fears hide in your darkness? Who do you
              need to share them with to make them smaller?

<u>5. Read:</u>

Page 176   Starting with, "Jesus stood back up and together they continued their meandering toward the dock." Ending with, "'It's all part of the timing of grace…'"

Question: How often has God tried to talk with you about the same topic? At some point, have you looked back and been able to see how many times He tried to tell you something? What does Jesus mean by "the timing of grace?"

<u>6. Read:</u>

Page 177-178 Starting with, "'It is a picture of my bride, the Church…'" Ending with, "…Jesus said with a chuckle."

Question: Is your church more like an institution or a living breathing community? What part do you play in your church? How do your expectations and/or involvement foster one type of church or the other?

<u>7. Read:</u>

Page 180   Starting with, "'If you try to live this without me…'" Ending with, "'…and together we'll watch it grow.'"

Question: When you are sinking, do you call on God? How do you let Him save you?

<u>8. Read:</u>

Page 180-181 Staring with, "Mack began to put on his socks and shoes." Ending with, "'You are free to love without an agenda.'"

Question: How do we keep God within us as we face the daily struggles of life on this world? Is it our job to change the world? Do we expect that our act of love to others will change them as well?

9. Read:

Page 181-182 Starting with, "'Mack, I love them." Ending with, "'…into my brothers and sisters, into my Beloved.'"

Question: Is it all as simple as just letting Jesus love us?

Comment

As with a spouse or a friend, maintaining a relationship takes an effort. It requires work, especially if it is to remain healthy. This means that the act of relating is a continuous process. In this chapter, Jesus is telling Mack just this; that the desired relationship is part of an ongoing process. One of the steps along the way is that we are to hand over our worries to God. A six-year old has little trouble relating to God because she doesn't carry all of the baggage that life puts on adults. We need to find our inner child by handing over the stress and worries of life to God. If we can hand over a little piece of our burdens everyday to God, our relationship will continue to prosper.

"The timing of grace," what a wonderful thought. Though God is with us always, and His grace awaits us, we don't realize the impact of His grace until specific moments in time. As the relationship is a process, we continue to learn the lessons God has for us and as we begin to recognize and embody each lesson, then we realize the grace that has been awaiting us. Working at maintaining a healthy relationship with God will continue to bring us the rewards of grace.

Each person has their own world, or sphere of influence. Some are larger than others, but that is not relevant. It is not our burden to change our world. However, by being with God we will impact our world simply by how we relate to those in it. Let others see that you have God in your soul and that will begin the change He has planned for your world.

Chapter 13

1. Read:

Page 185   Starting with, "He took another and sat back to savor it." Ending with, "Mack sat in silence, unsure what she meant or how to respond."

Question: What did God mean by saying that if Nan were there it would have been perfect?

2. Read:

Page 185   Starting with, "'Mack, just because I work incredible good out of unspeakable tragedies...'" Ending with, "'...but where there is suffering you will find grace in many facets and colors.'"

Question: Think of a time of tragedy or difficulty in your life. Where was grace then? How do you go about looking for grace in the midst of bad times?

3. Read:

Page 186-187   Starting with, "'Because that is what love does...'" Ending with, "'...that one day – that today – you will walk across.'"

Question: Reflect upon a time that you were stepping down a path of learning. When has God worked on a lesson for you over time, through many efforts? Are you in the process of learning something from Him now? Is there a way to expedite this learning process?

4. Read:

Page 187-188   Starting with, "'Lies are a little fortress...'" Ending with, "'If you had told her, maybe she would be here with us now.'"

Question: What lies do you tell yourself? What do you withhold from others? What would complete and open honesty be like?

5. Read:

Page 188-189   Starting with, "Papa's words hit Mack like a punch in the stomach." Ending with, "'...and that will be a greater miracle than raising the dead.'"

Question: What opportunities in life do you miss by withholding the truth? Are you able to ask loved ones for forgiveness? How does that heal you? At the chance of losing Nan if he comes clean, how can Mack put faith into God and tell the truth?

6. Read:

Page 190   Starting with, "'If only it were that simple, Mackenzie.'" Ending with, "'Love that is forced is no love at all.'"

Question: What does that last line mean, "Love that is forced is no love at all?"

7. Read:

Page 190-191   Starting with, "'Also,' she interrupted, 'don't forget that in the midst of all your pain and suffering...'" Ending with, "'...but then complain that I actually love you enough to give it to you.'"

Question:	From a humankind perspective, what have been some of the results of freedom of choice? From your own personal perspective, what have been some of the results of freedom of choice?

8. Read:

Page 192	Starting with, "'Like I said, everything is about him.'" Ending with, "'…but it is the nature of love to open the way.'"
Question:	What did God want from the very beginning of creation? What does Papa mean by saying she is "fully reconciled with the world?"

Comment

This chapter is all about reconciliation, though on several fronts. First, it deals with the comparison of sets of records. In the case of the story, comparing what Mack let's himself believe to be the truth and what God, and ultimately, Mack, knows to be the truth. We are challenged with eradicating what we rationalize as being the truth and living by what really is true.

The second message is simply pertaining to salvation as the result of atonement.

Another definition of reconciliation would be the end of estrangement, caused by sin, between God and us. When we are not truthful to ourselves, and then others, we are not truthful with God. Lies, or the omission of truth, are sins. Sin separates us from God. Reconciling those behaviors will help us remain close to God. In essence, we need to be in harmony, within ourselves relating to our adherence to truth, to others, and to God.

Chapter 14

1. Read:

Page 195-196   Starting with, "Mack nodded that he understood and turned the canoe toward the distant shore…"
Ending with, "He could see her point well enough."

Question: How do you learn to hear the Holy Spirit? How can we better avoid "mistakes?"

2. Read:

Page 196-197   Starting with, "'Mackenzie.' Sarayu seemed to rise up into the air." Ending with, "'…you don't want to trust them more than me.'"

Question: How does the phrase, *"Paradigms power perception and perceptions power emotions"* relate to judgment or the act of judging other people or circumstances?

3. Read:

Page 197-198   Starting with, "Mack allowed his oar to turn in his hands as he let it play…" Ending with, "…but rules will never give you answers to the deep questions of the heart and they will never love you.'"

Question: To you, is being a Christian just following a set of rules? What is the difference between a person that just follows the rules and someone that has Jesus living in them? Do you know of someone that has Jesus in their being? How do you get to that point?

4. Read:

Page 201   Read: "When the others stopped laughing, Mack continued. 'You know how truly grateful I am for everything, but you've dumped a whole lot in my lap this weekend. What do I do when I get back? What do you expect of me now?'"

Question: What did Mack say wrong?

5. Read

Page 205   Starting with, "'Let's use the example of friendship...'" Ending with, "'...or the responsibilities of a good friend.'"

Question: How can you stay in the verb, meaning in the active relationship state, instead of in the noun, meaning creating and enforcing laws and rules?

6. Read:

Page 206-207 Starting with, "'The trouble with living by priorities...'" Ending with, "...in and out and back and forth, in an incredible dance of being.'"

Question: What needs to change in your life to make all of this happen?

Comment

Life is like a path we walk, coming up to branches left and right that we can decide to walk down or not. It is the Holy Spirit that helps to guide us down the most productive path. However, if we are mistaken in what we hear from the Holy Spirit, or simply neglect the message, God is still waiting for us to listen again and He will meet us on the path where we are. Our path leads us to opportunities to bring Him to others. If we miss a turn, we miss the rewards that that opportunity would have brought us; the pleasure in touching God in another person. God will take care of those in the situation we missed, but it will be us that will miss the touch of God at that time.

Without complete truth and honesty within ourselves, our perceptions are tainted. This, then, will create emotions that are false to the moment. The better we are able to understand our motivations, either self-centered or God-centered, the better our perception will be and therefore our reaction and involvement to the moment.

Living "in the verb" is really action yet to happen, and a situation that we are to encounter with open eyes, open mind, and open heart. Living "in the noun" is really already having a preconceived notion, to have already characterized a moment, a person, a relationship, yet to happen.

This chapter is quite a bit about living in the moment, with the loving eyes of God directing our anticipation and reception. Living in the moment is not about lists of priorities or pyramids of responsibility. Instead, it is that mobile with all aspects of life equally revolving around you, with God, in the center. It is the wind of the Holy Spirit that moves parts of the mobile into and out of your view to be interacted with as they happen.

Chapter 15

<u>1. Read:</u>

Page 209   Read, *"You can kiss your family and friends good-*
                  bye and put miles between you, but at the same time
                  you carry them with you in your heart, your mind,
                  your stomach, because you do not just live in a
                  world but a world lives in you."

Question: Who do you carry in your world? How is your
                   relationship with all the members of your world?
                   How do you expand your world?

<u>2. Read:</u>

Page 213   Starting with, "'Yes,' Sarayu nodded, or at least
                  that's what Mack thought she did." Ending with,
                  "'…the richer the colors of that relationship.'"

Question: Are you aware of the uniqueness of each
                   relationship you have? Do you try to save on
                   emotion by categorizing several relationships the
                   same? How can you foster new curiosity in
                   yourself to enhance current relationships and find
                   new ones?

Comment

Having God in your life puts you into an active state. We are to
continue to strengthen our current relationships. We are to expand
our world, our sphere of influence by initiating new relationships.
We are to understand that every person, every relationship is
unique and therefore the sharing of God will be different, and
differently rewarding, with each one. We are to pursue the essence
of God in each person we meet, and to share God's essence in us
with them. A strong relationship with God can only make us more
curious to see how God relates with every other person.

Chapter 16

1. Read:

Page 221   Starting with, "As he mulled it all over and considered what he had learned..." Ending with, "...wondered what these changes would mean for Nan and him and his kids, especially Kate."

Question: How does having God in your life change your relationships with those you love?

2. Read:

Page 222   Starting with, "'There was no way to create freedom without a cost...'" Ending with, "'...but that doesn't mean I can't use if for good.'"

Question: Is Papa's second answer, "not an option for purposes that you cannot possible understand now," enough of an answer for you to move past any terrible incident? How do you get to the point of trusting God enough that you put aside the quest for a tangible answer, accepting that it is for a greater purpose than what we might understand?

3. Read:

Page 224   Starting with, "Now there was no holding back as hot tears poured down his face..." Ending with, "His voice trailed off."

Question: God wants to redeem those who have done wrongs to you, however, He asks you to forgive them. How do you forgive them? Where is justice?

<u>4. Read:</u>

Page 224-226   Starting with, "Papa waiting patiently for the emotions to ease." Ending with, "'That's the only way true forgiveness is ever possible.'"

Question: Does forgiveness mean forgetting? Can those two coexist? If not forgiving someone maintains a form of relationship, even if unhealthy, then does forgiving that person begin to change that relationship? Are we sometimes duty bound to maintain our hatred for someone that has done us, or a loved one, wrong? Papa says that we "have no duty to justice." How do we release that desire?

<u>5. Read:</u>

Page 227   Starting with, "'Wow!' he said hoarsely..." Ending with, "'...you may well know this man in a different context one day.'"

Question: Describe the process of forgiveness.

<u>6. Read:</u>

Page 228   Starting with,"'I did, but I told you I had something to show you...'" Ending with, "'...this crying and blubbering like an idiot, all these tears,' he moaned."

AND

Page 230   Starting with, "Papa unwrapped what Sarayu had sent with them..." Ending with, "...Mack muttering under his breath, 'I forgive you...I forgive you...'"

Question: In the first passage, Mack tells Papa "thank you" when told that they are there to return Missy's body. Would those be your first words under these circumstances? In the second passage, as he carries Missy's body out of the cave, Mack says over and over again, "I forgive you." Would those be your words at that time?

Comment

This chapter puts rights and justice against forgiveness. There is a fine line between the high level of self-esteem required to perform sacrifice and service without the pursuit of gain and the level of self-worth that encourages us to hold ourselves higher than others, that we have rights that have to be addressed, that no matter what the wrongs we perceive, we are due justice. With God in us, we won't feel entitled to be treated or judged by others in a manner of our choosing. We are fortunate to receive grace from God which fosters a wonderful relationship of love. We are to empower that feeling of love through us and wrap others in it. There is no room in that blanket for people's assumed rights and measures of imposed justice. To love is to actively forgive moving forward, not halting in the past with grudges and shortcomings.

Chapter 17

1. Read:

Page 231   Starting with, "Even though Mack carried the burden of Missy's body back to the cabin…" Ending with, "This was clearly the sanctuary of a master craftsman."

Question: Is this not an analogy; to give your burdens to Jesus because he is better able to carry them, He is the master craftsman? What burdens do you still carry?

2. Read:

Page 235   Starting with, "'I'd love to be with her.' He smiled at the thought." Ending with, "'…my purposes are accomplished and nothing will ever be the same again.'"

Question: Are you important? How do you touch your world? Do you let the Holy Spirit guide you as your actions impact those in your world?

3. Read:

Page 235-236   Starting with, "Now Sarayu stood in front of Mack and spoke…" Ending with, "In one moment, Sarayu's words opened up a new vista into Kate's struggle."

Question: How is it that now Mack is able to see the obvious cause to Kate's troubles? In what situations do you need to stop your selfishness to see the obvious to help those you love?

Comment

It is one thing that God thinks that you are important. It is quite another to get caught up in thinking that you are important, and measure that importance. Live with humbleness. Don't keep score of the moments that you think you've impacted other people with your character or beliefs. Instead, take pride in the fact that God does think you are important and does use you to convey His love to those in need. That sense of pride is to be really conveyed as thankfulness to God for allowing you the rewards of imparting His love to others.

Get out of your own head so that you can perceive the needs of those around you, those that you love. Serve them, not you.

Chapter 18

1. Read:

Page 242   Starting with, "Mack reached up and touched his friend's face." Ending with, "'He said,"Tell Willie that I'm especially fond of him.""'"

Question: How prepared are you to hear the words, if someone were to tell you, "God told me to tell you that He is especially fond of you?" What would the ratio of joy to guilt be in your reaction? Comfort to fear?

2. Read:

Page 243   Starting with, "The full story of his weekend, or day as Nan kept reminding him..." Ending with, "...whatever had happened had greatly impacted and changed her husband."

Question: When telling others of God in your life, how convincing are you? How much effort do you put forth to ensure that others believe you?

3. Read:

Page 244   Starting with, "Mack reached out his hand and Kate took it." Ending with, "But we'll learn together. Okay?'"

Question: How do you enable another person to seek and feel forgiveness, even when they don't know how to ask for it?

Comment

Like many songs out there today, we should live like we might die at any moment. Meaning, that we should be prepared to meet God now, knowing that we have done everything we can to be in sync with Him in our lives. We should have all of those conversations that we are waiting the right moment for. We should show the glory of God in our lives every time we are with someone. We should leave nothing undone. Living is an action. Living with God is an action. Do not wait or hesitate to show God through you. There is no time. The time is now.

After Words

<u>1.</u> <u>Read:</u>

Page 247-248   Starting with, "And Mack? Well he's a human being that continues through a process of change…" Ending with, "…crafted masterfully by invisible hands of love."

Question: Mack changed. Can you change? The changes in Mack "caused quite a ripple through his community of relationships – and not all of them easy." Are you ready for the consequences, good and bad, from the change to let Jesus live within you?

<u>2.</u>

Question: Who is the Willie in your life? If you don't have one, why not?

Comment

Enjoy the ripples! Share them with the Willie in your life.

CPSIA information can be obtained at www.ICGtesting.com
Printed in the USA
LVOW040832240412

278894LV00006B/59/P